Financial Strategies And Tips

Making and Saving Money In Today's Economy

Volume I

Melina Cooper

Table Of Contents

Introduction

Melina Cooper is an expert when it comes to finances and looking for ways to save. If you are looking for new, creative money making and saving methods, she has numerous books on various topics and subjects to guide anybody out of debt and into financial freedom and security.

Financial Strategies And Tips Volume I is just a beginning point, please look for her second edition Financial Strategies And Tips Volume II for a complete overview to your financial freedom.

For more of Melina Cooper's books, please conduct a search on Amazon using her name.

Prepare For Many Changes by Adjusting Your Budget

In times of economic uncertainties, people look for ways to save money and cut back on their monthly expenses. Just as the local economy can change at any moment, so can life. You may suddenly find out that you are expecting a new addition, or maybe retirement has snuck up on you. Changing your habits and sticking to those changes can be the hardest part of the process. As people, we often get stuck in our ways and thus, getting out of old habits can be a challenging process. The rewards, however, are well worth the effort.

One adjustment that will bring immediate results is changing your eating habits. By eating more home cooked meals, you can cut back on your monthly food costs. Start by bringing your own lunch to work instead of ordering out each day or resorting to fast food. Oftentimes, we fail to plan ahead and get into the habit of just going out to lunch rather than packing ourselves a sandwich or leftovers from dinner. While you may be supporting local businesses by eating out each day, you are certainly not doing your wallet any favors. It pays to also take it one step further and start eating most of your meals at home. This does not mean that going out to dinner or ordering a pizza every once in a while is off the table. However, eating out a few times a week can really start to add up.

Many people like to argue that it is too expensive and time consuming to cook your own meals at home. This could not be further from the truth. If planned correctly, you can actually save a lot more money following this route. Each week, create a list of the things you need and see how much money you can save on these items. Clip coupons, shop at stores that have sales and choose generic brand items. It also helps to create a meal plan so that you do not find yourself tempted to order out. This will also help you reduce waste as each item you buy has a purpose. Whatever money you do wind up saving, put the extra in a jar. Keep accumulating money each week until you have enough to buy or do whatever it is you desire. This will ensure that the item or trip (for instance) is paid for outright and not placed on a credit card.

Another area that you can save money in is your utility bills. The simplest thing you can do is turn off lights when you are not in a room. Try using your dishwasher only when you have a full load, and keep the thermostat turned down a little. If possible, try purchasing a programmable thermostat. These handy devices regulate your home's temperature and can be set to automatically lower the temperature when you are out of the house. This works for both heating and air conditioning. By just implementing these few tips, you can lower your energy bills each month.

Cell phone and cable bills are another area where adjustments can usually be made to save money. Today, there are literally thousands of different cable channels. While most of them come included in the basic package, many people opt for premium channels because they play the latest movies. The truth is that most of these channels replay the same film over and over again. Take a moment and look at your current cable package and evaluate whether or not you truly need these channels. The same thing goes for your cell phone bill. If you find that you consistently have leftover minutes each month, then switch to a lower usage plan. Text messages and data plans can also be lowered or eliminated altogether if you never use these features.

It will take a great deal of determination and willpower to cut back on these things. It is never easy to make changes as we grow accustomed to these luxuries. However, when you are expecting a life change, change may be necessary.

Thinking Of a Family Pet?

It seems that just about every home has at least one pet nowadays. They truly are a part of the family and bring so much joy to their owner's lives. However, pets are not free and come with a great deal of responsibility and expense. You need to ensure that you can really afford to care for them properly. There are a few things that you should take into consideration before deciding to add a pet to your family.

Whether you prefer the "purr" of an independent cat, the loyalty and companionship a dog brings, or some other little furry creature, there is no doubt that pets have become a major part of the family unit. They act as our best friends, risk their lives for us in times of danger and remain loyal to us until their last breath. Pets offer an unconditional love and forgiveness that is hard to come by with humans. So, if pets have so many great benefits, why is it that every family is not enjoying one?

Aside from allergy reasons, people refrain from getting pets because they can be expensive. Sure, they may be adorable, but there is no way around the fact that you are committing to care for the pet for their entire life. This means that you first have to pay to acquire the pet, and then you must ensure that you can afford to take care of them thereafter. Food, veterinarian visits, vaccinations, grooming and toys can all be very expensive. Pets are really no different than people. This is why it is important to approach the topic of adding a pet to the family in the same way you would if were you considering having a child. Unfortunately, there are thousands of pets that wind up in shelters or euthanized simply because their owners simply could not afford to care for them anymore.

Consider This Before Bringing Home a Family Pet

What kind of pet do you want? Are you thinking about a puppy, kitten, iguana, hamster, or some other creature? Each animal has its own set of needs. Even within the same species, each type has its own considerations. For example, a large dog might not be suited for apartment living as it needs plenty of exercise. Different types of pets are also prone to certain illnesses that may wind up costing you more than you can afford.

What kind of supplies will you need to ensure that you are ready for your new pet? Most people are aware of the costs of acquiring a pet, but they fail to consider all of the supplies they will need. A puppy, for instance, will need toys, bones, a crate (for housetraining), a leash, a collar, grooming supplies and a visit to the veterinarian. When you are in the market for a pet, you will also want to consider that the pet will eventually need to be spayed or neutered. The initial costs of acquiring a pet can easily cost you a couple of hundred dollars on top of the purchase price. These are certainly some factors to consider.

What are the long term needs of the pet? In other words, how much will it cost you to maintain your pet? Among these expenses are food, grooming, treats, toys, litter and yearly vaccinations. If you acquire your pet while they are still a baby, you need to consider the fact that they will be growing over time. Eventually, you will need to pay more for their food and they will need regular check-ups with the vet. This is to ensure that your pet lives out a long and healthy life.

If your family is considering more than one type of pet, you can weigh the pros and cons of each one to see which one will suit your financial situation. If you find that you just simply cannot afford it right now, adding a pet to the family may just have to wait. The research that you carry out will provide you with a future goal that you can work towards.

Cost Efficient Ways to Reduce Your Credit Card Debt

Many people today struggle with credit card debt. Unfortunately, having to carry around this extra burden can really prevent you from moving on in life. If you do have a large amount of credit card debt, you may be in a hurry to get rid of it. The quicker you can pay off your debt, the better your credit score will be. This will also allow you to begin saving more money each month, and reduce the amount of stress in your life. While you may want to eliminate your debt quickly, it may be better to instead focus on the most cost efficient way to reduce your debt.

There is no one-size-fits-all solution in this case. One method may prove to be the most cost efficient way to reduce debt for one person, but too burdensome for another. This will all depend on the amount of debt you have, the interest rates associated with these debts and the assets that you currently have. Below are a few possible methods to help you reduce your debts in a cost efficient manner.

Consolidate Your Debts

In some cases, a debt consolidation loan is the best option. If you qualify for this type of loan, be sure to check out what the interest rate is. You can then compare the interest rates on your credit cards and the interest rate of the loan. In most cases, you can save money by taking out a debt consolidation loan as banks tend to have much lower interest rates. Once you have paid off the credit cards, make sure that you cut them up. The last thing you want to do is put yourself back into the same situation again.

Cash In Your Savings

Do you have a savings account? If so, how much interest are you earning on that account? Take this number and compare it with the amount of interest you are paying on your credit card. If your credit card interest is higher than the amount you are earning on your savings account, you may want to consider cashing it in and using it to pay down some of your credit card debt. Once you have wiped away your debts, you can once again begin building a savings. Without monthly credit card payments, you accumulate savings much quicker.

Consider a Home Equity Loan

If you own your home, you may be able to take out a home equity loan to reduce or eliminate your credit card debts. Depending upon the interest rate and current market, this may be a sensible solution. Just remember that this option is similar to a debt consolidation loan. Once you have paid off your debts, make sure you do not run them up again. This will only force you into having to pay off a loan and credit card debt at the same time.

Paying More than the Minimum

Consider cutting your expenses in other areas to make more than the minimum monthly payments each month. In most cases, this is the cheapest and most effective way to reduce your credit card debts. If you have to, get a second job, sell your car, or move to another home that is less expensive. The quicker you can get out of debt, the more money you will have to save each month.

If borrowing from a bank is not an option for you, you can also consider taking out a loan from friends or family. If this is not an option either, you may need to take drastic measures. This may mean having to take on extra work, selling some of your belongings or moving. While these require commitment and change, you will wind up with more money and less stress in the long run.

Clipping Coupons: Strategies to Save You More at the Store

Manufacturers offer coupons to consumers as an incentive to try their product. If you are not using coupons, you are missing out on hundreds of dollars in savings each year. Let's take a look at a few effective strategies to help you make the most of those newspaper and magazine coupons.

Every Sunday, the local newspaper is littered with coupons for food items and home products. Manufacturers often add advertisement inserts with coupons on the bottom to entice you to buy their product. So, if the savings are that easy to find, why is it that more people are not using coupons?

Some people are actually embarrassed by the idea of using coupons. The truth is that 'couponing' is not an indicator of poverty or a person who is overly frugal. Coupons save you money, and everyone can benefit from saving money. The manufacturers of these products also receive tax breaks for offering these types of promotions, so you are not harming their business either. There is no reason not to take advantage of these savings!

Are you new to the idea of using coupons?

Use coupons in conjunction with promotions that are going on in-store. Most supermarkets hold weekly sales. You can often find their deals in the Sunday or mid-week newspaper. If you find a coupon for fifty cents off of a loaf of bread and you see that your local supermarket will have bread on sale for $1.50 on Wednesday, you can use that fifty cent off coupon on Wednesday to receive even more savings. Most grocery stores offer some kind of rewards card nowadays. They are free to obtain and often offer exclusive savings on their brand name and generic items.

Only clip coupons for items you use. This should be a given, but many people cut out coupons for items that look intriguing. Remember that when you are hungry, anything and everything will look enticing. Try to resist the temptation of buying items just because you have a coupon. This really is not going to save you any money. Instead, use coupons for the items that you use the most. For example, look for coupons for milk, meat, toothpaste or bread.

You can also save big by doubling your savings. Many grocers run promotions where they will double coupons up to a certain amount. Try to do your shopping during this time. This will allow you to save double the amount you would have otherwise. If you have a coupon for an item that you have been waiting to try, this is the best time to do it.

In the same manner that you want to be sensible utilizing coupons when they are double or triple savings, you also should study the coupon cycle. There is typically a twelve week cycle that coupons run on. When the Sunday paper has their listing of items for sale, you want to hold onto those coupons as those items will be most expensive right after the item has just been promoted by coupon. These tips and many more can be found on various websites that teach the most effective ways to go 'couponing'.

You can also find coupons online. 'Couponing' has become an internet phenomenon. There are a plethora of websites that list current offers and printable coupons for hundreds of different items. Coupons are often sorted by category to make browsing easier. This is similar to the old coupon boxes that you would find in grocery stores. Check online for your restaurant that you might be visiting as there are often available coupons in those venues as well.

Coupon clipping is one of the easiest ways to save money at the store. Instead of throwing out the circulars in the Sunday paper, be sure to go through them with a fine tooth comb and clip away. Make sure to check the expiration dates on your coupons to make sure that you do not miss out on the savings.

Recovering From a Student Loan Default

College is an expensive endeavor. For most people, taking out student loans is the only option they have to further their education. Each year, the price of college tuition goes up by a substantial amount. This just leads to more young individuals having to take out more student loans just to cover their education costs. In hard economic times, people often find it hard to make their monthly payments. As a consequence, they often default on their loans.

What Does Defaulting Mean?

If your loan payment is late or missed, it is considered a delinquency. Generally speaking, nine months of missed payments would put your account into default status. Essentially, this means that you have just stopped making payments on your loan. Each time you take out a student loan, you are making a commitment to repay the funds. You are obligated to hold up your end of the deal. If you stop making payments, you break your agreement with the lender.

So, what are the consequences of going into default mode? For starters, the Department of Education in your state will send you a letter notifying you of this default. From that point on, you will also be responsible for paying any fees associated with trying to recover the debt.

Other Consequences of Defaulting on Student Loans

Garnished Paychecks: As a result of your failure to make payments on your student loans, the lender may take necessary steps to have your paycheck garnished. Most agencies have to go through court proceedings in order to request a garnishment. However, the Department of Education does not have to jump through these hoops. They are able to take up to fifteen percent of your disposable income.

Tax Refund Eliminated: The Department of Education will notify the IRS of your default and you will lose the tax refund you normally receive each year. The money that you would otherwise receive will go straight to paying off your debts.

Legal Action Can Be Taken: The financial institution can sue you for the money you owe them.

Benefits Reduced: You may wind up having your social security benefits reduced.

Professional Licenses Revoked: You may also lose any professional licenses that you obtained through your education.

As you can see, there really is no way to get out of paying back your student loan debt. In one way, shape or form, they will get their money back from you. The best thing you can do is try to negotiate some kind of payment plan that is comfortable with both parties. This is a far better solution than defaulting on the loan, which also has a negative impact on your credit. If you are already at risk for defaulting, take the time to look for a suitable repayment option. Taking out a debt consolidation loan or negotiating a new repayment plan can help you avoid default.

Downsizing to Save Money

Because of hard economic times, many people are making major changes in their lives. At the end of the day, this is actually a good thing. Lowering your costs each month is always a good thing. One of the most drastic but effective ways to reduce your cost of living is to downsize your home.

If your children have gone off to college or now have families of their own, you may find yourself living in a big empty home. Having more room than you really need is an indicator that you can downsize. Consider the idea of moving into a smaller home or condominium. Before you make a final decision, take the following things into consideration.

Condition of the Local Housing Market: In many areas, it is still very much a buyer's market. Just because you are considering a smaller home does not mean that you have to give up all of the amenities you enjoy now. Small homes can have generous sized kitchens, big backyards, wrap around porches and walk-in closets. Look around for homes that offer these extras for reasonable prices.

Location: Are you comfortable with moving out your current city? If you stay in the same town, your tax rates will likely be the same. Property taxes are sometimes based on the city or the county and not necessarily the property itself. Look to see if there are any advantages to staying in or leaving your current location.

Managed Properties: You may not want to move to a home that requires a great deal of work to maintain if you are nearing retirement age. Mowing the grass and general home improvement tasks may become difficult as you age. Consider moving into a condominium. The maintenance fees paid each month go towards the upkeep of the property.

Low Mortgage Payments: Everyone likes to save money. Compare mortgages of homes you are considering to what you are paying now to see the savings. If possible, look for mortgages with interest rates that will allow you to save between $200 and $300 each month. The savings can be put away for retirement or used for vacation.

Lower Utility Payments: Smaller homes require less energy to warm and cool. If you live in a larger home with empty rooms, you are just wasting money on your heating and cooling bills each month. Moving into a smaller home has the potential to save you a substantial amount of money in this department.

Making a Profit Off of Your Home: While it may be a buyer's market, it is still possible to make a profit from the sale of your home. How old is your home? How well have you maintained it? Are you located in a desirable neighborhood? If your home has a number of features that are attractive to buyers, it will not be such a chore to sell it when you decide to downsize.

If you are thinking about downsizing your home, you must first consider whether or not it is a sound financial decision to do so. Using the points above, you can make an informed decision.

Newly Divorced? Financial Tips to Keep You Afloat

When a couple decides to dissolve their marriage, they lose more than just a partner. One of the parties will lose their home and both will lose an extra paycheck. Most families today live off of two incomes. Once a divorce becomes final, both parties will find themselves being the sole provider for themselves and their children. An audit of your current expenses needs to be done so that you can determine what you can live on. Gather up all of your bills and determine what your total is each month. Be sure to include food and gas expenses as well.

If you find that your current home or apartment is too expensive, you have a few options. If you are renting, you can downsize and move to a smaller apartment. If you are committed to a mortgage, you can either refinance, or you can put your home up for sale. While it may be difficult to give up your home, the sale will likely yield you profits that you can put away as savings.

The first year is likely to be the hardest as you will still be making plenty of adjustments. For immediate results, try to scale back on your cable and cell phone bills. Most of the time, we have far more channels that we actually watch. At this point, you can go over your current package and see if there are any cheaper packages that are better suited to your viewing habits and then eliminate any cable boxes that you do not need. Cell phones can often be reduced down to just the basics. Cut back on the extras like unlimited text messages and data usage. You will soon find that a lower plan will save you a great deal of money each month.

Adjustments will also need to be made in the food shopping department. If you had been in a relationship for a long time, you may be used to purchasing larger amounts of food. It only makes sense to buy smaller quantities of the foods than you are used to buying. If you see a good sale on meat or produce that can be frozen, feel free to stock up. Be sure to make a list, check local flyers for sales and clip coupons to ensure that you are getting the best deals possible. Eat the vast majority of your meals at home and bring your lunch to work with you. This will save you a substantial amount of money each month.

In some cases, even when you do everything that you possibly can, you still cannot make ends meet. In this case, you may need to take on a second part-time job to offset your expenses. If you have children, this can be especially difficult on them and yourself. However, you need to ensure that you can provide for them. Just remember that where there is a will, there is a way. You may even be able to find a part-time job that allows you to work from home.

Making changes to your lifestyle can be very difficult. When you add a divorce into the mix, it becomes even more challenging. However, there is no way around the fact that you are now responsible for yourself and your children if you have them. This means that you have to make necessary adjustments to your budget each month and curtail your spending habits. Make cuts where necessary to allow you some flexibility.

After the Honeymoon: Financial Tips for Newlyweds

Getting married is an exciting, stressful and joyful time. Now that you have found the love of your life and have made a commitment to each other, life becomes a little more complicated. Once the honeymoon is over, adjustments to a new life must begin. However, you do have one advantage that others do not. You can begin your new life together with a clean slate. If you take the necessary steps, you can prepare for whatever life may throw at you and set yourself up for a long and prosperous marriage.

The very first thing you should do is sit down and make a budget together. Create a list of all of your bills and your weekly expenses. If one party comes into the marriage with debt, the best option is to consolidate that debt and pay it off as quickly as possible.

Be wary of credit card use. They are wonderful to have in case of an emergency situation, but when abused, can create a lifetime filled with debt and stress. The problem with credit cards is that they are so easy to use and people are now in the habit of just swiping away when they make a purchase at the store. There is a good chance that even your morning coffee is charged to a credit card each morning. Most people fail to think about the fact that interest is tacked onto their bill each month. Try to keep the number of credit cards to a minimum and make sure that it is tucked far away in your wallet for emergency purposes only.

Another thing that should be high on your list is a joint savings account. By adding money into this account each month, you get into the habit of saving for big purchases, vacations and retirement. You can start by making small deposits and eventually add more over time. This will help you create a nice little nest egg. That nest egg can eventually be used to purchase a home, take a vacation or start a family. This will also help you avoid using a credit card in an emergency situation.

Only use cash when purchasing items at the store. This is one of the most important tips for newlyweds. When you begin a new life together, you want to make sure that you do things right. Using cash for purchases will provide you with two major benefits. For starters, you will be able to see how far you can stretch your money. Also, when you only use cash to make a purchase, you are far more likely to think about each item you buy. Once your wallet is empty, you will have no money left to spend. This will help you avoid impulse buying.

It is not uncommon for newly married couples to experience financial difficulties at the beginning of their marriage. This is especially true if the two of you have never lived together. When you establish a monthly budget and use spending habits that are healthy, you can avoid arguing over money. Providing that the two of you have little debt, you can enjoy living the life that you want and enjoy doing things together.

Setting Financial Goals

While everyone has different goals in life, there is one thing that we all can agree on; financial security is of the utmost importance. When the economy is in a rocky state, you need to do everything you can to keep your financial future stable. This will not be possible if you do not implement goal oriented strategies.

Reasons to Set Financial Goals

Goals are not exclusive to the career department of your life. When you have goals in your life, it gives you direction and something to work towards. It becomes difficult to make plans for anything without them. When it comes to the financial department of your life, having financial goals will ensure that you have appropriate funds for important life events such as retirement, college and vacations.

In order to begin setting up some financial strategies, you need to think about what your life goals are. These are not just short term life goals, but long term. What do you want to do with your money? Determining your life goals is the first step.

Creating Financial Goals

Put it in writing. If you want to take your goals seriously, write them down on a piece of paper. It is far too easy for the details to get sketchy over time if you do not take this important first step. Once you have them written down, you can modify them as needed. They do not have to be in any particular order. You just want to ensure that you have them on paper so that moving on to the next step becomes easy and clear.

Be specific and detailed. Take a look at what you have written down. If your goals look something like "I want to buy a new house," you are being too vague. Buying a home is something that everyone aspires to do. How is this vague phrase going to help you create a strategy? You need more information. A better goal would be, "I want to save up $10,000 for a down payment on a home within two years." This gives you a deadline and an amount to work towards. At this point, you can begin thinking of ways to set aside money to reach this goal in time.

Turn big goals into smaller ones. Large goals, like the one mentioned above, can be broken down into smaller, workable goals. When your budget is tight, the idea of saving up $10,000 may seem impossible. However, if you change that big goal into smaller, workable ones, it suddenly becomes possible. These smaller goals will help you reach your long-term goal on time and in a way that makes sense to you. For example, you could say, "I want to save $416 each month. Within one year, I will have saved $5,000. At the end of the second year, I will have saved $10,000 to put down on my new home."

Do your homework. Start by reading money magazines and researching different money saving strategies. Speak with a financial advisor if you can. They will be able to give you advice on the best route to reach your goal with minimum effort.

Always evaluate your plan. Read over your goals every few months and see if anything has changed. Evaluate whether or not you are still on the right track towards meeting your goal, or if you need to make some adjustments. Sometimes unforeseen circumstances prevent us from reaching our goals on time. Adjusting your goals allows you to stay on track.

If you really want to achieve your financial dreams, you need to work smarter and not harder. By implementing the right strategies, you can enjoy a life of financial security and freedom.

Money Saving Tips for Seniors

Life does not get easier with age. In fact, it typically gets more difficult. Once you stop working, the only thing you have to live off of is the money you have saved for your retirement. Therefore, you need to work harder to ensure that you are getting the most out of your money. Below are some tips on how you can stretch your dollar further.

Discounts for Seniors: Many establishments offer discounts for seniors nowadays. Take advantage of them whenever you can. When eating out with your family, choose a place that offers discounts to their senior patrons. If you are unsure if an establishment offers a discount then simply ask. You may be pleasantly surprised. Remember that you may need to show identification in order to receive the discount.

Shopping for Groceries: Some grocers also offer discounts for senior citizens. This may be a certain day of the week/month, or it may just be a part of their everyday policy. Plan to do your shopping on the day that this special discount is offered, and do not forget to bring your coupons with you. This will help you save even more on your food bill each month.

Consider Public Transportation: Although you may have a license, it may not be economical for you to drive everywhere. Gas is expensive, and prices are projected to continually rise. Consider taking public transportation. Many cities offer senior discounts on their bus fares. If you must, you can park your car and ride the bus around the city. Some churches also offer van pick-ups for seniors on Sundays. Sign up for this service if it is available.

Entertainment: Most entertainment facilities offer discounts for seniors. This includes movie theaters, museums, gyms, zoos and more. If you are planning on going out over the weekend, take a look into these places. This will allow you to do the things that you love without having to pay full price. If you do not see a sign for a discount, you can politely ask if they have one.

Online Communities: You are certainly not the only senior in the world. There are many just like you that are looking for ways to live more frugally. Thankfully, there are many websites and forums online where seniors can gather and share information on local places that offer discounts for seniors. This includes leisure activities, exercise facilities, shops and more. Ideas can also be shared here on creative ways to save money. This is also a great place to make some new connections and friends with other seniors who live nearby.

Shopping For Clothes: When it comes to shopping for apparel, seniors are never forgotten. There are many stores that have special days when seniors can receive a percentage off of their purchases. Keep an eye out for these sales and plan to go shopping on these days.

A senior discount is just one way for businesses to show their appreciation for all that you have given to society and your family. This can save you money when you dine out, shop for clothing and food, purchase medication, renew car insurance, or go out for a day of fun.

How Seniors Can Save on Prescriptions

As you approach retirement age, you may have a number of concerns about your future and how you will make ends meet. It is best to cut expenses wherever possible in order to ensure that your golden years are stress free and enjoyable. You spend your entire life worrying about money so the last thing you want to do is stress about finances during retirement. For most seniors, the biggest cost they incur comes from their monthly prescriptions.

There is no denying that the pharmacy industry is a billion dollar one. Drug manufacturers put millions of dollars into research and developing new medicines. This cost is often reflected in the prices of these live-saving medications. Prices can still be high even with insurance. This becomes even more of a concern if you are retired and on Medicare.

Below are some ways that seniors can immediately begin addressing this issue. Even if you are not on any medications right now, there is no reason not to start planning on how to deal with this situation, should it arise.

Focus on your diet. Unfortunately, many senior citizens do not take into consideration the food that they are eating. This is especially true for those who are living in nursing homes or by themselves. Many forget to eat during the day. This unhealthy habit can have a detrimental effect on your health later on down the road. A lack of nutrition, or malnutrition, can lead to a plethora of medical issues. Seniors are even more vulnerable to these issues. This can lead to osteoporosis, dental issues, organ failure and heart disease. Any one of these conditions will require medication and doctor visits. By eating healthy and regularly, you improve your chances of having a healthy future.

Exercise regularly. Many healthy seniors enjoy happy lives that are free from medications. This is because a healthy body does not need medicine. During the cold season, a healthy body is far more efficient at fighting off the illness than a body that is malnourished or mistreated. Many seniors shy away from exercise because they feel they are just too old. The truth is that exercise can provide you with plenty of energy. It improves your quality of life and your longevity. It also keeps your muscles and bones strong. A short but brisk walk around your neighborhood each day will suffice.

Take advantage of drug samples. If your doctor recommends that you begin taking an expensive medication, you may want to ask for a sample first. Doctors frequently give samples to their patients that are supplied by the drug manufacturer. Trying out the medication first will allow you to see whether or not it is a good choice for you. This will save you from having to pay for a month's worth of medication that you will never use.

Get in touch with drug manufacturers. Many of these companies understand that tough economic times make it difficult for people to be able to afford expensive medications. If your medications are necessary but you are unable to afford them, you may want to contact the manufacturer. They can often put you in touch with someone who can enroll you in a special program that is designed to help seniors with their medication costs.

Do not be afraid to buy generic. Ask your doctor to prescribe you generic forms of your medicine. These can be filled at your local pharmacy for a much cheaper rate. Some medications are only four dollars each month.

If you have concerns about the costs of your medications, the aforementioned are a few ways that you can save money on the cost of your prescriptions.

Living on Less: Tips for Seniors

Living on a fixed income is never easy. It does not matter whether you are new to retirement, or have been retired for a number of years; a limited income presents a number of challenges. No doubt you have spent decades saving and spending money. Now is the time to sit down, create a budget and stick to it. This budget should not only make your dollars work harder, but it should also allow you to live life comfortably. Saving money in your golden years is no different than saving money in years past. Turning off lights when you are not in the room and keeping your thermostat low are two habits you should continue. However, there are a few other ways that you can save money and make sure that your retirement is free of stress.

Believe it or not, being a senior comes with many advantages. A large percentage of retailers offer a senior discount. In some cases, they offer fifteen percent off your purchase. Senior discounts can be found at museums, movie theaters, Broadway shows, restaurants and clothing outlets. One advantage of being retired is having the freedom to shop whenever you want. This will allow you the time to make your list ahead of time and visit all of these stores in one day.

When shopping for groceries, opt to buy the generic store brand items. These are often of the same quality as name brands, but cost much less. When non-perishable items like paper towels and toilet paper are on sale, buy them in bulk. In addition to looking for sales, you should also start clipping coupons. Be sure to shop at your local grocer whenever they offer double coupons to maximize your savings. If you are unsure of whether this is offered at your local market, ask a customer service representative.

For recreational activities, you may want to consider your local senior center. You will be able to mingle with others that are your age and enjoy weekly events like bingo, dancing, movies and even casino nights. There is always something new and fun to do. Senior centers only charge a small fee to participate in these activities, so you can enjoy a night out without having to spend a lot. All the while, you can develop new friendships with other seniors who share the same interests.

Just because you have to live on less, it does not mean that you have to sacrifice the things you love. If you can keep an open mind, you can do all of the activities that you have always enjoyed at a fraction of the cost. Many seniors find that a good way to save on costs is to sell their car and rely on family or public transportation to get around. Having a car can be convenient, but it can also be very expensive to maintain. If you find that you can live without your car, you can save yourself quite a bit of money each month.

It can be challenging to live on a fixed income – especially during the first few years of retirement. Being a senior citizen comes with many benefits, so take advantage of them whenever you can.

Living a Happy Frugal Life

There are many people that talk about living a frugal lifestyle and the many benefits that come along with it. Yet still, there are many people that look down upon those who practice this. Being frugal does not mean that you have to sacrifice everything you love. In fact, your life really does not have to change at all.

Most people do not have the luxury of being able to afford whatever they want, whenever they want. Everyone can benefit from saving a little extra money. The problem is that when we have the money for an item, we do not think twice about paying full price. Living frugally changes this mindset and not your lifestyle.

Oftentimes, people associate the term "frugal" with being cheap. This is simply not true. When a person is "cheap," they skimp out on things. Being frugal means that you are buying a good or a service that is of high quality, but at a cheaper price.

Each time you choose to pay full price for an item or a service, you fail to take into consideration the financial consequences. For instance, why would you pay full price for a wheelchair when you can get the same item for half the price through Medicare or your own private insurance company? Sure, it takes a little more effort, but the savings are well worth the time.

People who love to travel may worry that they have to give this up during hard economic times. It is perfectly possible to travel if you do so frugally. There are many websites that offer discounts on hotel, airfare and car rental fees. These discounts are often substantial. Dine in fancy restaurants and stay in four star hotels for a fraction of the cost.

There is no doubt about it that living a frugal lifestyle takes some effort and research. It requires you to analyze each discount and deal carefully to ensure you know exactly what you are getting. This goes for special travel offers, car rentals, clothing sales and eating out.

If your child needs money to go out with their friends over the weekend, you can hold a yard sale. This gives them an opportunity to learn some organizational skills, and decipher which items they really need and which ones they can do without. This also allows them to interact with their neighbors and teaches them the value of money. At the same time, you can enjoy a cleaner home and they earn the money they need to go out. It is a win-win for everyone.

Everyone should give frugal living a try. Doing so does not mean that you have to give up all of the things you love. This just gives you an opportunity to do these things in a smarter way.

Reducing Funeral Costs

The topic of death is not something people are comfortable talking or thinking about. Naturally, we might wish we could just avoid this part of life entirely. When a loved one passes away, it can be a very difficult time for those who were close to the person. Nonetheless, arrangements must be made. Taking care of these concerns ahead of time can make this time less stressful and allow you to make smart decisions when you are faced with that decision.

While death is not a pleasant topic to talk about, it is one that needs to be addressed at some point. If there is a prolonged illness involved, there may be more time to plan things out. However, there are situations when a death occurs suddenly and cannot be prevented. In either case, funerals must be arranged. Even if you have a general idea of what will be needed and the costs, there are some things that you may not anticipate.

Consult with a local funeral director: These individuals deal with these situations every single day. They can explain the entire process to you from the prepping of the body, to the viewing, service and the burial. This is just a basic outline of the process, but it gives you some kind of idea. With this outline, you have something to go on.

Choose service vendors: Did you know that you can use other vendors for some of the services associated with a funeral? Remember that funeral homes are just like any other business and they make a lot more money when you use them for everything. However, you do have the option to choose a different place to hold the viewing, hire your own floral company, hold the gathering wherever you choose and also purchase your headstone from somewhere else.

Burial method: Caskets are expensive. While they are great for use during the viewing, they will be put into the ground afterward and remain there indefinitely. Cremation is also an option. This will not require a casket, but an urn instead. A simple casket can be used for the viewing and you can even purchase your own urn. This also eliminates the need to have to buy a plot.

Military death benefits: Veterans often qualify for death benefits along with their life insurance policies. Be sure to ask about it.

Private family hour: There is no requirement that you have to have the casket present during the family hour. If you choose, you can save the casket viewing for the day of the formal service. The family hour can then be held in your own home or a local church.

Family gathering: If you are a member of a church, you can inquire about holding the gathering there after the service. Ask other members of the church if they would like to help out with the food arrangements. If every person brings a dish, the gathering can turn into a potluck with more than enough food to feed everyone.

While planning a funeral is not exactly a pleasant task, it is necessary. Using some of the above mentioned tips, you can plan a beautiful service that will not break your budget.

Making Funeral Arrangements Ahead of Time

Just about everything in life can be planned ahead, and funerals are no different in this way. Taking the time to plan out the details before your time comes can help relieve some of the stress your grieving loved ones will experience.

There is no need to leave the planning of your own funeral service up to your loved ones when you can plan out every last detail yourself. You can even pay for it all before your time comes. This relieves the financial burden that is often put on loved ones when their family members pass away. You can even plan out the eulogy if you wish.

The very first thing you should consider is where you want your final resting place. There are many people that opt to purchase a family plot so that each member of the immediate family has a place. Plots can also be paid for in installments. This means that if an accidental death should occur, you will be covered.

Caskets are another thing that you need to take into consideration. Shopping for caskets is a lot like shopping for a new car. You do not necessarily need to be buried in a wooden box, but you do not have to get the Porsches of caskets either. Consider the monthly price of the casket you are considering before you commit to purchasing it.

In some cities or states, a burial vault must be used to bury the dead. Essentially, these are boxes made from steel that hold the casket. In this case, people are buried on top of one another to keep the integrity of the plot intact. If this is a requirement where you live, remember that you will be responsible for that cost as well. There is no need to spend a great deal of money on a casket as it will be protected by the steel walls.

Flower arrangements also need to be taken into consideration. A funeral wreath is the conventional route, but there is no set rule that says you must purchase one. You can also choose to have a few strategically placed vases filled with beautiful flowers. This will look just as nice and can then be taken home by family members to be enjoyed. This part of the process can be arranged outside of the funeral home.

Embalming and presentation are two more details that need to be planned. Of course, if you choose to be cremated, you can avoid this part altogether. The casket and viewing can also be eliminated as the urn can simply be placed with portraits of the deceased. As far as presentation goes, you can choose to be dressed in one of your favorite outfits instead of buying new clothes.

The biggest advantage of making all of these arrangements ahead of time is that you can choose whatever services you want and pay for them so that others do not have to.

Getting Back on the Financial Track

In today's world, it is very easy to get off track with your finances. It is estimated that most American homes have an average of $7,500 worth of credit card debt. To make matters worse, most people owe more on their homes than they are actually worth. However, this does not mean that your financial ship has sunk. By working with a budget, you can get yourself back on the right track.

The first step may seem a bit obvious. You must determine exactly how much money you have coming in and how much you have to pay each month. Gather up your bills and separate them into groups. Place bills that are urgent together, such as the mortgage or rent, utilities, credit cards, etc.

If you are having issues paying your energy bills, contact your providers. Many companies will offer their customers a budget plan wherein you pay half of the balance you owe up front and then are billed the rest each month. It is okay to continue paying just the minimum on credit cards for the first few months. From there, calculate the costs of gas and food.

In some cases, you may find that your budget is just stretched to its limits. At this point, you will have to tighten your belt strap and do without extras for a few months. Eat meals at home, make your own morning cup of coffee, and skip those nights out. Just by doing these few things, you can start getting yourself out of the financial hole you dug for yourself. Remember these changes are only temporary.

To save money on food, make a list before going to the store. Also, plan your meals each week. Sticking to your plan will save you a great deal of money. Make sure to use coupons as well to save even more money. If you can, cook a few casseroles during the week. This will provide you and your family with a few meals.

Lower your thermostat when you are out of the house and before going to sleep. If you have the means, start replacing your regular light bulbs with energy efficient ones. They really do save quite a bit of money. Turn off any appliance that is not in use and unplug them.

There are many families that become overwhelmed and go overboard when budgeting. They fail to realize that just these few simple tips can make a real difference. Be smart about how you use your money and put anything extra away for a rainy day or future emergencies.

Tips on How to Stay Afloat After a Lay-off

If you are among the many that have recently been laid off, you may find yourself unprepared for this sudden loss of income. If you qualify for unemployment, this can most certainly help you through the first few months. While they will not be able to sustain the life you once had, they will help with some of the anxiety a lay-off brings. However, until you are able to gain employment again, times will be a little more difficult.

If you rent your home or apartment, you may be in a better situation than someone who owns their home. You can start by appealing to your landlord to see if they would be willing to give you a reduction on your rent for a few months. If not, you can search for local apartments or homes that are affordable. If you do own your home, you can try refinancing if you have a partner who is employed.

Making the effort to reduce your utility bills can also make a big difference. As mentioned earlier, programmable thermostats can have a huge impact on your monthly bill. Just lowering the temperature at night or while you are away will provide you with major savings. And again, turn off the lights when you are not in the room.

Cable can also be an expensive luxury. While you do not need cable to live, it is nice to at least have the basic channels to enjoy some kind of entertainment during your nights in. Lowering your current package can help you save a lot of money each month. The same thing goes with your cell phone. Get rid of any features you do not need and be sure your minute limit is realistic.

When shopping for groceries, make a list prior to leaving home. Check out the local flyers to see which items are on sale in your local stores. This can actually help you create menus each week and almost create your list for you. Cut out any coupons you see for items you actually use and buy generic brands all while sticking to your budget each month.

Being laid off is no walk in the park and will require you to cut back on your expenses. The good news is that most people live well beyond their means, so reigning in those extra expenses can teach you a lot about what you really need and what you can do without. Learning how to budget properly and living within your means will help you stay afloat during the best of times and the worst of times.

The Cost of Being a Smoker

Cigarettes now come with warning labels that educate buyers on the adverse effects of the product. Regardless of these warnings, people still continue to smoke. The numbers of reasons to quit smoking are endless and go beyond just the health risks. A pack of cigarettes can cost between five to twelve dollars. If you smoke one pack a day, you are spending nearly three thousand dollars each year on cigarettes. If you smoke two packs, that is six thousand dollars a year which is quite a bit of money. When more than one person smokes in the home, the costs can become astronomical.

Smoking is more than just a burden on your wallet. It also effects the way that you spend your time and takes a number of years off of your life. The list of complications and illnesses associated with smoking are limitless. Emphysema, bronchitis and pneumonia are not uncommon. Many smokers wind up developing lung cancer as a result of their habit, and many times, the cancer is detected far too late and becomes nearly impossible to reverse.

The nicotine in cigarettes is responsible for the powerful addiction associated with smoking. Experts compare it to heroine in this department. This is why so many people try to quit but fail. Even when someone has quit for many years, just one cigarette can bring them right back into their addiction.

Smoking affects the size of your wallet, your health and the health of those around you. Second-hand smoke is just as deadly as first hand smoke. This is why many children who live in homes with smokers wind up with asthma or other bronchial issues. Just take a rag and wipe down the walls in your home. The yellow residue should be proof enough that this habit is terrible for your health and the health of your loved ones.

There really is nothing beneficial about smoking. If you have tried to quit in the past but have not found any success, you can try a support group. Take every measure possible. Your money, your family's lives and your own health are on the line.

Financial Tip for Teens: Making Money with Recycling

We are all well aware of the need to protect the environment. After all, the Earth is the only planet we have. Recycling is a great way to reduce waste and prevent landfills from being littered with items that take hundreds of years to breakdown. Recycling is also something that teenagers can do to make some extra money.

When you recycle items, you collect and reuse items rather than buying new ones. If a product is recyclable, it will have a symbol on it that resembles a triangle made from arrows. You can take this opportunity to teach your teenager about the importance of going green and doing their part to better the environment. Along the way, they can make some extra money. Below are some ideas:

Start up your own local recycling service: If your town does not have a recycling program, your teen can go around the neighborhood and collect recyclables from neighbors. Start by only accepting particular items so that it does not become overwhelming. Unless your teen has their license, this will require you to drive them around. Have them put up flyers that state the prices and the pickup times. You can store the recyclable items in a truck or storage rooms until you are able to get to a recycling center. Contact the facility to see if they have requirements for how the items are bundled.

Sell recycled items online: Many electronic retailers will pay customers for old computer parts. Collect motherboards, monitors, keyboards and other computer peripherals. These items can be sold to these retailers. Just be sure to check what they offer for the items before you begin collecting them. It may or may not be worth your time.

Create new items out of recycled materials: Teenagers can be very creative. With recycled materials, there are no limits to what they can create. These items can be sold at local flea markets or on eBay for some extra cash.

Open a thrift store: Not all recyclable materials need to be sent to a recycling center. Many people who are looking to save money will purchase second hand items. Furniture, clothing, music and appliances that are gently used can be sold. Hold a yard sale to sell the items or have your teen set up their own online storefront. People are always on the lookout for good deals on second hand items or items that are hard to find like classic records.

If you allow your teen to take the initiative, they have the potential to make a great deal of extra money. Along the way, they will learn the value of a dollar and many important life skills.

Please look for **Financial Strategies And Tips Volume II** by Melina Cooper.

www.ingramcontent.com/pod-product-compliance
Lightning Source LLC
Chambersburg PA
CBHW051300170526
45165CB00004B/1786